Still *the* Night

Still *the* Night

160201

THERESA TOVA

Still the Night
first published 1998 by
Scirocco Drama
An imprint of J. Gordon Shillingford Publishing Inc.
© 1998 Theresa Tova

Scirocco Drama Editor: Dave Carley
Cover design by Tétro Design
Photograph by Paul Martens
Author photo by Bill Hume
Production photos on pages 55, 66, 75 and 89 by Trudie Lee
Production photos on Pages 10, 48 and 79 by Cylla Von Tiedemann
Printed and bound in Canada

We acknowledge the support of The Canada Council for the Arts and
the Manitoba Arts Council for our publishing program.

Canadian Cataloguing in Publication Data

Tova, Theresa
    Still the night
A play.
ISBN 1-896239-36-6
    1. Title.
PS8589.O92S75 1998   C812'.54   C98-901169-0
PR9199.3.T6175S75 1998

For Bob, David and Tara: Your love allows my desire to fly.
For the two Brynas: These stories were born out of a compassion
and a need to understand.

About the Staging

Still the Night is a memory play set in three time periods: the 1930's to early 1940's, the 1970's and the present day. As in a dream, the set should float in space. In the original production the set was a Chagall-inspired black and white playground where time and place could be shifted in the blink of an eye. Surrounded by scrims with exits available throughout, the set accomodated all locations without any shifting of scenery. A tall A-frame ladder centre stage reached towards the heavens and was used for trees, crosses, entrances and exits. There was a comfortable living-room chair on one platform and a trap door on another. The only physical props used were a photo album, a glass tea cup and saucer, a gun, a wash cloth which doubled for a baby and an apron, a basket and a sheet of note paper.

Tybele is the only character who speaks in the present. The same actress plays Tybele, Young Tybele, Bryna and Big Bryna. When Little Bryna enters she draws Bryna back into the past to become Big Bryna. Big Bryna almost always becomes the older Bryna when seated in her favourite chair. Both Big and Little Brynas are in their early teens in the 1930's scenes and age up to 50 years of age in 1972. The languages fluently spoken by Big Bryna include Yiddish, Polish, Russian, French and English. Little Bryna speaks very good Yiddish and a little Polish.

Cast of Characters

Actress One TYBELE (1990's)
                   YOUNG TYBELE (1970's)
                   BRYNA (Tybele's mother, 1970's)
                   BIG BRYNA (Bryna as a young girl, 1930's and 1970's)

Actress Two LITTLE BRYNA (Big Bryna's cousin)

Production Credits

Still the Night, a co-production of Tapestry Music Theatre, Theatre Passe Muraille and Tova Entertainment, premiered at Theatre Passe Muraille, Toronto, on October 31, 1996 with the following cast:

TYBELE, BIG BRYNA .... Theresa Tova
LITTLE BRYNA .... Liza Balkan

Directed by Anne Anglin
Set and Costume design by Mary Kerr
Musical Direction and Arrangements by John Alcorn
Lighting design by Andrea Lundy
English Translations by Hindy Nosek-Abelson and Theresa Tova
Stage Manager: Kathryn Davies

The final draft of *Still the Night* was premiered as a co-production of Tapestry Music Theatre, Alberta Theatre Projects and Tova Entertainment at the Martha Cohen Theatre, Calgary on October 12, 1997 with the following cast:

TYBELE, BIG BRYNA .... Theresa Tova
LITTLE BRYNA .... Liza Balkan

Directed by Tom Diamond
Set and Costume design by Mary Kerr
Musical Direction by Wayne Strongman
Musical Arrangements by John Alcorn, Wayne Strongman
and Theresa Tova
Lighting design by Bonnie Beecher
English Translations by Hindy Nosek-Abelson and Theresa Tova
Dramaturge: Melanie Joseph
Stage Manager: Colin McCracken

Still the Night is based on a script originally improvised by Theresa Tova and Liza Balkan with the dramaturgical work of Anne Anglin.

Theresa Tova

Theresa Tova is a writer and performer who has created a sensation with her first play, *Still the Night*, which was nominated for three Betty awards and won four Dora Mavor Moore awards, including Best New Play. Born in Paris, France, Theresa immigrated as an infant with her parents to Calgary, where she attended private Yiddish school and started her acting career. A Gemini and Dora nominated actress, she has since gone on to star in television, film and stage. She recently toured the U.S. in *Ragtime*, performing the role of Emma Goldman, all the while continuing to pack theatres with her concert show "From Belz to Broadway". As the *Toronto Star* proclaimed, "Theresa Tova is an artist Canadians should celebrate."

Theresa Tova as Bryna. Inset: Bryna, 1947.

ACT ONE

Scene 1—Stories

(Present day. The song "Telling Stories".)

TYBELE: *You've told me your stories for so many years*
           And still the telling has only begun
           These stories half hidden in memory and shame
           They've fought to survive and they've won.

They're like old friends. I have loved these stories but I have also fought with them. As a child my dreams were haunted by them. My mother's stories—my bedtime stories were told in the middle of the night... And like my mother I had to find my own way to survive. One afternoon I came home from school and found my mother in the living room. She was crying...she wasn't angry. She was gentle, almost peaceful. I'd never seen her cry like that before. She was sitting with a package of pictures in her lap. An agency had found distant relatives living in Australia...after the war even fifth cousins were a big deal. They had an old photo album with pictures of my mother and her family from before the war. For the first time I had faces to place in my stories.

(In the 1970's, afternoon.)

YOUNG
TYBELE: Oh Mama, How old are you? ...Thirteen? Look at your hair... You look like me...except for the hair. Ha, ha...oh let me see that one. What are you doing? You're all dressed up like a Chicago gangster?

Al Capone aha ha…ahh look at you in the country.
Who's that with you on the horse? your cousin?
She's the one you were with? Oh! Mama look at
you, I smile just like you, don't I? Yes I do… Look at
your smile. I've never seen you smile like that
before?…That's my grandfather?…He's scary…he
is…he's so stern…

(YOUNG TYBELE sits down in the 1970's chair to become:)

BRYNA: Look at him, Mordche Chudy, that's your Zayde.
He was a fine man, a refined man. Not like your
father, intelligent. From the intelligentsia of Warsaw. A free thinker. Oh you see how tall he was,
good looking. When he walked down the street
people noticed. And every Saturday night he
would take my mother, get dressed in their finest
and they'd go in a carriage to the opera, and he
loved my mother… He was a shoemaker. The best.
We had a factory right in the bottom of the house.
Oh he had, let's say, 10, 12, sometimes more men
working for him in that factory. No matter what we
didn't have we always had good shoes. I showed
you how to tell a good leather shoe didn't I? My
father showed me. What you do? First you go into
a shoe store and you ask the salesman, "Tell me, is
this a good leather shoe?" and of course he's going
to say yes. Because he wants to make a sale. So
you… make sure you ask him again, yes? "Tell me
is this a GOOD leather shoe? Huh? You're sure?
Good." And you take this nice leather shoe and
you squish it just like this, right in front of his face.
I love seeing his mouth just drop. Hey no problem!
If it's a good leather shoe…you see it springs right
back. Not so good, there's a little line a crack, but
don't show him. And if it isn't leather? Well he can
throw it out. You know the good thing about that.
It teaches him not to lie.

(Stands up in the 1990's)

TYBELE: The first time I was in a holocaust play, I realised
how much that world already belonged to me.
Every night on stage, we would say the Kaddish, the
prayer for the dead. We would say the names of
those who died. I of course had my own names.
Mordche Chudy...Tybele Chudy.

(Violin.)

I was named after my grandmother Tybele. It means
little songbird. And I was in the middle of my mono-
logue when he came to me... Tybele...

("Belz" underscore begins.)

My grandfather, he called my name.

Dertsayl mir alter,	Please tell me zayda
Dertsayl mir geshvind	I really want to know
Vayl ikh vil visn alles atsind	Everything you know
Vi zeyt oys dos shtibl	
A house that used to shine	
Tsu blit nokh dos beymele	
Can the tree in bloom be mine	
The little house is old	
Tsevaksn mit mokh un groes	
The roof is leaking through	
The windows without glass	
The porch stands all bent	
On poor, crooked walls	
It's not the old home	
You remember at all	
Der ganik is krum	
Tseboygn di vent	
Di volst dos shoyn mer	
Gornisht derkent	

He was calling me. He was saying thank you Tybele.
Thank you for remembering. He understood. He
knows how much these stories are really mine now.

(Over to the 1970's chair, to become:)

BRYNA: That was downstairs. Upstairs? Oy, the house was
                always so full of people. Me, I had my little cousin
                Bryna. She used to visit. Bryna yes? Two cousins,
                the same first name. But Little Bryna she was sim-
                ple a country girl. Me, I loved the city. My Mama
                she was from a rich family, we had a maid...very
                very elegant. She set such a beautiful table. And my
                Tata he had important visitors. They had dinner
                parties with English diplomats, Polish Diplomats
                and Russian Politicians...

Scene 2—At the Dinner Table

> *(BIG BRYNA joins LITTLE BRYNA at the dinner*
> *table, 1930's.)*

BIG BRYNA: Yes mama.

LITTLE
BRYNA: *(Overlapping.)* Yes...

BOTH: Bryna!

> *(Looking at each other.)*

BIG BRYNA: You go first.

> *(Being served.)*

LITTLE
BRYNA: Adank.

BIG BRYNA: Adank mama. *(Pointing out the diplomat.)* He's a
                Democratic Socialist...from Russia.

LITTLE
BRYNA: A what?

BIG BRYNA: Dobrey Dyen tovaritch... A little Russian yes.

> *(Both eat while listening to conversation.)*

Oh but Tata I thought that the Trotskyists were
Russian? NO, no sir I know that! Lenin is the father.

LITTLE
BRYNA: Lenin is your father?

BIG BRYNA: The father of Communism, stupid. That's why Tata
                    makes me go to a Christian school. So I can under-
                    stand what's going on in the world, right Papa? Yes
                    so I can understand politics. Do you even know the
                    name of the Pope?

LITTLE
BRYNA: I...

                    (More eating and listening.)

BIG BRYNA: Oh do you hear what they're saying? There are
                    rumours flying around. Things are getting very
                    bad for the Jews. They're going to start branding
                    us? Oh Papa. You see my Tata he knows these
                    things...he's a Communist... He's been in jail.

                    (Diplomat asks LITTLE BRYNA a question.)

LITTLE
BRYNA: Hmm?

BIG BRYNA: Oh she wouldn't know that sir. No, no, Bryna, she
                    goes to a Jewish school. She doesn't know any-
                    thing.

LITTLE
BRYNA: Excuse me.

                    (Standing violin stops.)

                    I do know that it's Shevuot and at Shevuot it
                    should be dairy and not meat and certainly not
                    what? Farglivete feets? You can never eat jellied
                    feet ever! Where is the dairy? Where is the cheese
                    blintzes? Where is the cheese kugel? Where where
                    is the milkhik lokshen kugel? And at Shevuot there
                    should always always be rice pudding! And my
                    mama, my balabuste says that Marx was a JEW!

                    (BIG BRYNA slips back to the 1970's.)

BRYNA: You know, I never really liked Bryna that much.

The only reason we spent so much time together is because she always hung on.

(Both BRYNAs back to the 1930's.)

LITTLE
BRYNA: This is the best dress I have.

BIG BRYNA: Well tuck it in. You have to be better dressed to go shpatseern with Tata... Coming! Hurry Bryna. Tata won't wait for us.

LITTLE
BRYNA: Where are we going in such a hurry?

BIG BRYNA: Shpatseern. We do this every night after dinner. We get dressed properly and we go walking on the streets.

(Shpatseern music.)

LITTLE
BRYNA: Everybody's looking.

BIG BRYNA: Of course.

LITTLE
BRYNA: Look at that fur!

BIG BRYNA: That's Mrs. Hirszowicz, she's very rich. Good evening Mrs. Hirszowicz.

LITTLE
BRYNA: Look at that bakery.

BIG BRYNA: Crystal chandeliers.

(Percussion—danger.)

LITTLE
BRYNA: What are they doing to that rabbi?

BIG BRYNA: No, no stay here.

LITTLE
BRYNA: But cutting his peyes…they can't do that.

BIG BRYNA: Tata says you shouldn't wear kipas. Don't you understand it's not safe to look Jewish anymore.

> *(They both walk away. BIG BRYNA goes to her 1970's chair and she becomes:)*

Scene 3—At the Movies

        (1970's.)

YOUNG
TYBELE: Ma you want a gleiselle tai? I'll get a cup of tea for both of us. Oh and Ma I found the empty wrapper. Where'd you stash the chocolate? *(She sees that her mother already has the chocolate.)* Yes…I knew it! I'll turn on the TV. There's an American musical with Fred Astaire. God I love it when we sit together, sip tea and eat chocolate.

        (Sits to become:)

BRYNA: Don't chew! What the hell are you doing? Didn't I show you before. You don't chew chocolate you hold it… All right I'll show you again. You break a piece of the chocolate off yes? You hold it in your mouth… Don't chew…and you sip the hot tea through it… Just like that…right down you let it…another piece? …Now you can wait. Oh I love movies.

        (BRYNA, from the chair, remembers BIG BRYNA and LITTLE BRYNA at the movies, 1930's music.)

LITTLE
BRYNA: You've missed the part where she finds the note. Oh this is where she goes on stage. She goes on stage and she's in front of all those hundreds of people. And they ask her to sing something, but she doesn't know what to sing. And then she sees her boyfriend, she hears him in the orchestra…

> ("Yidl Mitn Fidl" starts to play and movie score
> continues under:)
>
> ...Arye mitn Bass
> Dos lebn is a...
>
> Oh its a wonderful movie. She's the best!

BRYNA: She's dressed like a shlob.

LITTLE
BRYNA: No, she has to dress up like a boy because she goes
with her father across the land and plays the fiddle
and she dresses up like a boy so no one will bother
her. But then she meets a Klezmer band and they
are wonderful musicians and there's one of them
who is very handsome...and she falls in love.

BRYNA: Molly Picon? She's no Ginger Rogers. I need more
chocolate. Excuse me.

> (BIG BRYNA joins LITTLE BRYNA.)

LITTLE
BRYNA: You almost missed it.

> (Song "Oy mame Bin Ikh Farlibt" begins.)

Oy mame bin Ikh Farlibt
Oy mame bin Ikh Farlibt
A Klezmer yingl mame getrayer
Ligt mir nor in zin
Ick vayn und lakh und vays nit mame
Oyf velkher velt ikh bin
OY
Oy mame bin Ikh Farlibt
Oy mame bin Ikh Farlibt
Khvolt di gantse velt arum genimen
Un tsugedrikt tsu zikh
Oy mame bin Ikh Farlibt

Oy I love him so, he was very beautiful but then he
met a beautiful woman equally as beautiful and I

was afraid that she would fall in love with him and he would fall in love with her...because why would he fall in love with me... I was dressed up as a boy and he wouldn't fall in love with me? ...no it was very sad...but don't laugh... Her if tsu lakhn... No, no lakh nisht fun mir...

BIG BRYNA: They're laughing at you...would you sit down?

LITTLE
BRYNA: I don't care. Oh, oh wait. This is the best part...they're on the boat...and look who's there? Her boyfriend...they're on the deck of the ship, and they're leaving now.

BIG BRYNA: They're going to America.

LITTLE
BRYNA: YES! and they kiss.

(Both girls embrace as movie ends.)

BIG BRYNA: Are you happy now? Can we go?

LITTLE
BRYNA: Oh no I want to see it again.

BIG BRYNA: Bryna! You saw it already three times.

LITTLE
BRYNA: Ya?

BIG BRYNA: Last week before? Come on let's go.

LITTLE
BRYNA: But I don't have enough money and I really want to see it again. Please...

BIG BRYNA: Well I'm not spending anymore to see it again.

LITTLE
BRYNA: But I don't have any more money.

(She starts to wail.)

BIG BRYNA: Wait, I'll show you… I get in trouble from you, I'm gonna kill you. When I say, go under the chairs quick.

               (LITTLE BRYNA starts to go.)

               Wait… *(Looks around.)* Now Down! *(Pushes LITTLE BRYNA under chairs.)* All the way in…sh…sh… *(Watching the usher.)*

LITTLE
BRYNA: Did he see us?

BIG BRYNA: No… I do this all the time…

LITTLE
BRYNA: You do?

BIG BRYNA: Last week I saw Cary Grant three times in a row.

LITTLE
BRYNA: I'm sure somewhere in the Torah this is very wrong.

BIG BRYNA: Nothing is wrong as long as you don't get caught.

LITTLE
BRYNA: Blessed is he the one and only…

BIG BRYNA: I can't believe I'm doing this for Molly Picon!

               (Coming out of hiding. To another moviegoer:)

               Hey hey my chair!

               (Covering their tracks with a lie:)

LITTLE
BRYNA: I lost it.

BIG BRYNA: Thank you.

LITTLE
BRYNA: I found it.

BIG BRYNA: No. No everything's fine now, thank you very much.

(The movie music starts again.)

LITTLE
BRYNA: Oh it's starting. Remember the dream? Where she's wearing that beautiful dress and then she turns into a boy again and she gets all sad when she turns into a boy.

BIG BRYNA: You really have to see Betty Grable.

LITTLE
BRYNA: Who?

BIG BRYNA: BETTY GRABLE! The one with the legs that go all the way up to her neck.

LITTLE
BRYNA: I don't care what you say. It's in Yiddish and it's Warsaw and she's Molly Picon…

BIG BRYNA: All right so it's in Yiddish, but look at the way she dresses. Like a shlepper, in boys clothes for god sakes. You know Ginger Rogers? You don't know Ginger Rogers. She dresses all in white—white hair, white face…beautiful gowns that wrap around her body she even has to walk with a kick her dresses are so heavy.

LITTLE
BRYNA: Oh wait wait wait. They're on the haywagon now.

(Song "Yidl mitn Fidl"/"Puttin' on the Ritz" begins.)

Yidl mitn fidl Arye mitn bas
Dos Lebn is a lidl vos she zayn in kas
Hey Yidl fidl shmidl Dos lebn is a shpas

LITTLE
BRYNA: *Iber felder vegn*   BIG BRYNA: *If you're blue and*
                                                 you don't
           a wagon full of hay   *know where to go to*
                                                 why don't
           There go two musicians   *you go where*
                                                 fashion sits
           riding on their way   *Puttin' on the Ritz.*

                                                 Different types who
                                                 wear a day coats
                                                 Pants with stripes
                                                 and cut away coats
                                                 perfect fits
                                                 Puttin' on the Ritz
                                                 Decked out like
                                                 a million dollar trouper
                                                 Trying hard to look
                                                 like Gary Cooper
                                                 Super dooper
           A chiddish Oy A question   *What?*
           Tell me who we are they   *Gary Cooper?*
           Yidl mitn fidl Arye with his bas   *Puttin' on the Ritz*
           Like is just a song   *Puttin' on the Ritz*
           why have such a face   *why have such a face*
           Hey Yidl fidl shmidl   *Hey Yidl fidl shmidl*
           Dos lebn is a shpas   *Puttin' on the Ritz*
           Dos lebn is a shpas   *Puttin' on the Ritz*

                        (In the 1970's.)
BRYNA: Life...is just a joke.

Scene 4—The Farm

(1970's card game with friends.)

BRYNA: My deal… All right…two ladies walk out of a deli. The one says to the other one, "Rukhelle look, look. Look across the street at your husband Max!" "Where?" "Dere! coming out of the florists…with a dozen roses? Eh Ruchelle! Hu Ha, Friday night roses." Ruchelle says, "Oy a brokh you don't know what it means." "Rukhelle what's your problem a dozen roses on a Friday night how can this be a tsooreh, a problem?" "You don't understand. It means I have to go home, I have to lie down, I have to put my legs up in the air…" "Rukhelle you don't have a vase?" Wait, wait, wait. Where are you going? Ladies please, before you go my daughter wants to show you how she learns Polish. Come on Tybele tell them what I taught you. Come on.

YOUNG
TYBELE: MA! …I only know a few words… Petsalvnye Dupe… Yap tvoya matt…

BRYNA: OOH yoo yoo what you can't stand a little dirt? Hoy…Tybele look at those ladies run! Huh? Don't ask! You told them kiss my ass and something to do with their mothers. You scared little shits! Run! Ha ha.

(She laughs and through laugh becomes:)

YOUNG
TYBELE: What are you teaching me? Ha ha. Mama can I ask you something? You know Marina and Lila and Bonnie, well they're all going to put in a little bit of

money. Actually it's Bonnie's mother's idea. And what they're going to do is they're going to buy us this series of books on um...menstruation...and you know...how things are really done. And so I was wondering if we could put in a little money for these books too?

(Sits to become:)

BRYNA: Sex? You want to know about sex? You know more than I do! Go get me a hot water bottle. Don't be in such a hurry to grow up Tybele. It doesn't get any better.

(On the farm, 1930's.)

LITTLE
BRYNA: Over there...that's where Zisl lives, there.

BIG BRYNA: That farm boy?... Has he kissed you?

LITTLE
BRYNA: Bryna!

BIG BRYNA: Has he?

LITTLE
BRYNA: Maybe.

BIG BRYNA: Maybe yes, maybe no, tell me. Does he kiss you the French way?

LITTLE
BRYNA: What?

BIG BRYNA: You know, with an open mouth.

LITTLE
BRYNA: Aghh!

BOTH: Aaah!

LITTLE
BRYNA: Like this?

BIG BRYNA: Mm. Hm. That's what they told me...

LITTLE
BRYNA: I hope it was a Jewish boy who showed you?

BIG BRYNA: Nobody showed me. How could they? I go to Christian school. When I walk past the Jewish school they all scream at me...call me names.

LITTLE
BRYNA: I'm sorry it's so hard for you... This year I'm too old to go to girls kheyder. So I have to work for the princess who owns the farm.

BIG BRYNA: The great madamskypoo.

LITTLE
BRYNA: Ahem. I milk the cows and I work in the fields. But only in the mornings. In the afternoon I have everything to myself.

BIG BRYNA: A farm. There's nothing to do on a farm.

LITTLE
BRYNA: We could go into town to sell beets.

BIG BRYNA: This summer in Warsaw Pesakh Burstein and Lillian Lux are at the Scala in *Gypsy Lover*. I hope we can go back soon. Tata says we have to wait until it's not so dangerous. My Tata was organizing meetings and marches. Mama had to go to the jail again to get him out...

LITTLE
BRYNA: Oh no!

BIG BRYNA: She paid them a lot of money. And she made him promise not to...oh, I'm not supposed to tell...

LITTLE
BRYNA: Tell!

BIG BRYNA: My Tata, he started sneaking men through our

house. Yes! important men. They stay with us the last night before they go underground.

LITTLE
BRYNA: Oh Bryna.

BIG BRYNA: That's how we got here. When Tata decided that we should also get out. Mama got us all dressed in three, four layers of clothing. With our best things on the outside. And we went for a walk just like always down the streets of Warsaw to the edge of the ghetto. And there through a crack in the wall a truck was waiting and the next thing I know we're here on the princess's farm, Ya...so we can start working for the madamskypoo too.

(The music for "Vi shlekht und vi biter" begins.)

How hard and how bitter it is
To live this life of drudgery
How hard and how cruel so base I could die
My stomach's in knots
And my heart is farklempt for sure
Go on and laugh all I do is cry.

LITTLE
BRYNA: *I come from peasant stock*
My blood boils good and hot
Kokht es all week long
Listen dear Mommy do
I want that madamskypoo
To find that the worst has gone wrong.

BIG BRYNA: *I would never let anyone make a fool of me*

LITTLE
BRYNA: *I know*

BIG BRYNA: *Though they all hate me these people that I meet*
I'll manicure my nails
And I'll paint them the deepest red
That way you can't tell
I've been grating the beets. Ah!

LITTLE
BRYNA: *I come from peasant stock*
                My blood boils good and hot

BOTH: *Kokht es all week long*
                Listen dear Mommy do
                I want that madamskypoo
                To find that the worst has gone wrong.

                (LITTLE BRYNA climbs up a tree.)

LITTLE
BRYNA: Yoo hoo!

BIG BRYNA: It's the only way you'd be taller than me.

LITTLE
BRYNA: Yes well you're not so tall.

                (BIG BRYNA lifts her over her shoulders.)

BIG BRYNA: Hey I've got a sack of Jewish potatoes for sale!

                (They fall down laughing.)

LITTLE
BRYNA: You can eat these mushrooms.

BIG BRYNA: Really?

LITTLE
BRYNA: Ahm. They're good.

BIG BRYNA: They're dirty.

LITTLE
BRYNA: No they're not, that's the earth. Peel off the skin
                and its good. No NO. Not that one. It's poison.

BIG BRYNA: What?

LITTLE
BRYNA: If it's thick on the bottom it's poison...don't.

                *(LITTLE BRYNA eats a mushroom and fakes
                poisoning.)*

BIG BRYNA: Bryna. Bryna!

                (LITTLE BRYNA starts to laugh.)

                You!

LITTLE
BRYNA: Ha ha... Look your father's wearing a skirt again!
                Ha ha.

BIG BRYNA: Ha ha. It's not funny.

LITTLE
BRYNA: Such an ugly Meeskeit. Meeskeit! Meeskeit!

BIG BRYNA: Don't laugh at him. He's going to the outhouse.
                And he has to dress up like a girl otherwise the
                neighbours will know that he's here.

LITTLE
BRYNA: I'm sorry...Sheyne Maidle...ha ha ha.

                (Shouting to Tata at the outhouse.)

                You know you have to sit down now! La la la la la.

BIG BRYNA: Don't make fun. Your father gets to go out of the
                house. Mine stays in the attic all day. If he had a
                dress that wasn't too small I think he'd actually
                look pretty good.

LITTLE
BRYNA   Very good for a girl.

                (Percussion; BIG BRYNA sees something.)

BIG BRYNA: Don't run, walk very slowly back to the house.

LITTLE
BRYNA: What?

BIG BRYNA: Nazis. They're coming!

LITTLE
BRYNA: Papa?

BIG BRYNA: He's just going down to talk to them. So my Tata
               can get back up into the attic.

               (Both girls watch.)

LITTLE
BRYNA: They've turned back down the road. They're tak-
               ing Papa with them!

               (Girls run into the house.)

               Yes mama? All right I'll go. I'll go after him.

BIG BRYNA: I'll go with…

LITTLE
BRYNA: No, we won't talk to any strangers. We'll wait for
               him.

BIG BRYNA: We'll wait until they let him go and we'll bring him
               back.

LITTLE
BRYNA: Yes mama it's all right. We won't eat anything
               don't worry.

BOTH: We're going to town!

               *(Girls make their way down the road into town.
               Music for "Vi shlekht und vi biter" comes up.)*

BIG BRYNA: It'll be all right.

LITTLE
BRYNA: *Friday after supper*
               After Kishkes mit Tsimering
               He'll come to visit me
               My dear sweet young boy

BIG BRYNA: *He'll kiss me*

LITTLE
BRYNA: *And he'll hold me*

BIG BRYNA: *And he'll grab every part of me*

LITTLE BRYNA:	*And I'll start to sing*
BIG BRYNA:	*'Cause I've learnt to enjoy*
BOTH:	*I come from peasant stock* *My blood boils good and hot* *Kokht es all week long* *Listen dear Mommy do* *I want that madamskypoo* *To find that the worst has gone wrong* *He says that we'll marry* *That he'll take us both away* *He says that we'll marry* *My dear sweet young boy*
BIG BRYNA:	*He'll put on his top hat*
LITTLE BRYNA:	*Oh how handsome can he be*
BIG BRYNA:	*And that high falootin Madam* *Can go on and die*

(The girls are now in the crowded town square.)

BOTH:	*I come from peasant stock* *My blood boils good and hot* *Kokht es all week long* *Listen dear Mommy do* *I want that madamskypoo* *To find that the worst has gone wrong*

(Boots land on the stage.)

LITTLE BRYNA:	Those look like Papa's boots. *(To passerby.)* Do you know where they took... Antshuldik mir. Do you know what happened to Leiser Nissenbaum... Excuse me where is the man with the boots?
BIG BRYNA:	Gje! Yest pen Pan zbootami?

LITTLE BRYNA:	Papa!... What... What?
BIG BRYNA:	They took him away...
LITTLE BRYNA:	What do you mean?
BIG BRYNA:	Bryna...
LITTLE BRYNA:	Where did they take him?
BIG BRYNA:	Bryna... We have to go now.
LITTLE BRYNA:	*(Together.)* Papa!
BIG BRYNA:	*(Together.)* Tata!

> *(They run home. LITTLE BRYNA exits with boots.)*

What are you packing? Are we going back now? ...No, you can't. You can't go back to Warsaw without me... Are you taking Mama? Then take me... I won't know what to do when the Nazis come back... Pretend that I'm Polish? they'll know that I'm not...the forest? I don't want to be with Partisans, I want to come with you and mommy... Please Daddy. Please take me with you... I'm not...I'm not strong... I'm not... Then Mommy you stay with me please. I don't want to be alone. I don't want to be alone!

> *(1990's.)*

TYBELE: It took me a long time to understand how even when I was with her, my mother was always alone. After the war in Paris she met and married my father, he was the perfect find... He had six brothers and sisters. She married his family as much as him. But my dad he was pretty good looking...

TYBELE: *(Con't)* anyway he was the last single brother left to
                 marry. Mom borrowed her wedding dress from
                 my dad's sister. Everyone borrowed it. All my
                 aunts wedding pictures are the same. My parents
                 didn't have to take their own wedding picture at
                 all. All they had to do was cut out the faces and put
                 in their own. After the pictures of my grandparents
                 found us I used to dream that I could cut out their
                 faces and paste them back into our lives.

                 *(1930's. TYBELE watches as LITTLE BRYNA en-
                 ters with a garland.)*

LITTLE
BRYNA: How many more weeks are you going to sit inside?
                 You're not in mourning Bryna. You can't sit shiva
                 for a father who isn't dead. Come out, so we can
                 play in the corn field, it's taller than you now... Oh
                 you have such a stubborn head...

                 (BIG BRYNA sees the garland.)

                 You want one. You can have one, no you have to
                 come out.

                 (Outside.)

                 See we have lots of flowers. You take your thumb
                 and you put it on the bottom. And you take another
                 one and you put it right through.

                 (Joins LITTLE BRYNA in 1930's.)

BIG BRYNA: I'll never do this...you make me a crown.

LITTLE
BRYNA: You'll need a big one?

BIG BRYNA: Aha, because I am Queen Princess. I am Madam-
                 skypoo.

LITTLE
BRYNA: Oh yes and I will milk the cow.

BIG BRYNA: Yes!

LITTLE
BRYNA: I will clean the flooring and I will do the beets.

BIG BRYNA: Do the beets!

> *(Sound of danger. Both girls see enemy soldiers on the road. They hide in the corn.)*

LITTLE
BRYNA: What are they doing?

BIG BRYNA: You see Tata was right. He said they would come back.

LITTLE
BRYNA: Let's go back to the house. Maybe they need our help. No no they're taking mommy! Where are they taking her...no no NO.

BIG BRYNA: RUN! RUN!

> *(They run through cornfields into the forest and end up huddled at the top of a tree.)*

Where does that path go?

LITTLE
BRYNA: It cuts through to the water where there's a boat.

BIG BRYNA: I can't swim.

LITTLE
BRYNA: There's a boat!

> *(They climb down and walk along the path until it splits in two.)*

BIG BRYNA: Which way?

LITTLE
BRYNA: I've never come this far before.

> *(Sound of an owl.)*

BIG BRYNA: If nothing is going right go left.

                (They crawl further into the forest.)

                I'm hungry.

LITTLE
BRYNA: I know. We'll find berries and mushrooms when
                it's light. Here's a pine tree, and feel...moss, it's
                soft. Here, Bryna lie down. Just like Moses in the
                wilderness. Pretend this is Succoth, this is God's
                house and he'll take care of us.

BIG BRYNA: We have to take care of ourselves now, Bryna; not
                God, you and me. We have to be strong. We'll go
                back when it's safer... We'll find my father and
                then we'll be all right.

LITTLE
BRYNA: And then we'll make shabes dinner, havdallah
                with a candle made from the three parts...and
                we'll light the candles and then we'll burn a piece
                of challah to give thanks, and bless the wine and
                eat a proper meal with lokshen kugel and kreplakh
                and...

BIG BRYNA: Cow's feet.

LITTLE
BRYNA: No you can't have that. Oh Lord you are mighty
                forever Thou revivest the dead, and art powerful
                enough to save

                *("Succoth" or "Geshem Nign" [Autumn Prayer]
                and "In Kriyuvke" [In a Hideout.] The autumn
                prayer for rain, signaling as it does the arrival of
                cold weather, serves for the lament of one ill-pre-
                pared for the rigours of the approaching winter.)*

                Thou Lord art Mighty forever, Thou revivest the
                dead, Thou art powerful to save

Ato Gibor l'olam
m'khaye mesima
torav I'hoshia

BIG BRYNA: *Hiding in a shelter think it over*
I'm so tired my eyes they won't stay open
With bitter tears that pour upon this forest floor
Will I ever see my home once more

Sing, sing your song full of pain
Sing to me your Yiddishn Nign
Sing, sing your song so full of pain
Will I ever find my home again

> *(They huddle together and fall asleep. Silence. Danger shocks the girls awake. They are surrounded by Polish soldiers. They try to run.)*

BIG BRYNA: Yesteshmee Polski. Nyet Jedem. We're Polish girls!

> *(BIG BRYNA is caught, thrown down and raped. LITTLE BRYNA scales up a tree. She is pulled down and raped in turn.)*

BIG BRYNA: Bryna!

LITTLE
BRYNA: Bryna!

> *(BIG BRYNA gathers her shoes and speaks to the soldiers who are congratulating themselves on their conquests.)*

BIG BRYNA: Look, look what you Polish soldiers did to Polish girls.

LITTLE
BRYNA: Polski!

BIG BRYNA: Don't say anything. You speak Polish like a Jew! Yestchemi glodni. Yestchemi wodi. We're hungry, so you give us food and water and then we won't tell your commander what you did to Polish girls.

Come we'll go with them. They'll feed us and then we'll run away.

(LITTLE BRYNA is pushed off by the men. BIG BRYNA is pushed back to her 1970's chair.)

Scene 5—Shopping

BRYNA: No. No. No. Grisha get off me goddamn you! You
              can take your snake and you put it somewhere else
              do you hear me? I'm not a piece of dirt anymore.
              Never! Never again!

              (Getting ready to leave the house.)

              Tybele, go put on a dress. My Tata would never go
              out with you looking like a bum. Every weekend
              the same thing, he goes to the shvits, the steam, he
              drinks whiskey with his shlepper friends and all of
              a sudden I'm a piece of milk herring. You make
              yourself better Tybele, promise me. And don't
              bring me home anything but a six foot Jewish Law-
              yer! It's just as easy to be a queen.

YOUNG
TYBELE: Ma, why are you walking so fast?

BRYNA: Five years of running you learn to walk fast.

YOUNG
TYBELE: But Ma I can't keep up!

              (She turns slowly.)

BRYNA: You want me to buy you a bra or you don't? Huh?
              This morning you're crying they're all making fun
              of you, you want a bra? So let's go. Into the store.

              *(LITTLE BRYNA joins BIG BRYNA in 1930's.
              Hands her a babushka for disguise.)*

LITTLE
BRYNA: Here. It's getting late. The soldiers said we have to
               be back to the camp with the supplies before dark.

BIG BRYNA: Then maybe you should walk faster. Where's the
               money?

LITTLE
BRYNA: There's only enough left for sugar. But we need a
               thread and a needle.

BIG BRYNA: It's all right. I'll talk to the man. You go over there
               and fast you get what we need.

               (As LITTLE BRYNA shoplifts:)

               Chaysht...proshe...chimozesh mi pomutz. Chemi
               zukra da take... Jinquee-e... Jinquee-e... From the
               farm down outside of town yes. Thank you. My
               cousin, she's very shy. We're just visiting. Jinquee-
               e jinquee-e...

               *(Both girls exit store. BIG BRYNA takes off the
               babushka and turns back to the 1970's store.)*

BRYNA: Don't worry I won't embarrass you ...Lady! excuse
               me, my daughter here, she thinks she's growing
               up. She doesn't need...she wants a bra. No she
               doesn't know what size. So measure her.

               (Measuring against her daughter's breasts.)

YOUNG
TYBELE: Mom do you have to really? Come on, not in the
               middle of the aisle! *(Being measured, arms up like a
               cross.)* Oh God!...36? Really?

BRYNA: That's your back. Your front, you wouldn't fit a
               triple A.

               (Back in the 1930's.)

LITTLE
BRYNA: We'll use one of their shirts for material.

BIG BRYNA: Where are they? Did they see you?

LITTLE
BRYNA: Shhh. When I left my soldier he was sleeping.

BIG BRYNA: Good. Now how I do this?

LITTLE
BRYNA: My mama showed me. You take material, and you
              cut out triangles and you sew them together.

BIG BRYNA: Really? How many?

LITTLE
BRYNA: (Measuring against BIG BRYNA's breasts.) Six.

BIG BRYNA: Damn. It won't tear...

              (LITTLE BRYNA pulls out a pair of scissors. Un-
              derscore to:)

              Where did you get those?

LITTLE
BRYNA: The store.

BIG BRYNA: So you are learning you little thief, ha?

              (The song "Avreyml the Pickpocket". BIG BRYNA
              continues cutting triangles.)

LITTLE
BRYNA: *I was left homeless young but clever*
              Poverty chased me out forever
              By thirteen years I tell you it's no lie
              In strange places far from mother's caring
              Dirt and hunger taught me to be daring
              But I turned out to be a real great guy

              I am Avreyml pickpocket and all round crook
              A skilled artist I could write a crook book
              The first time ever I remember still today
              I got busted just for stealing bread oy vey
              I don't hang out with those other crooks and snitches

> *I steal from cheapskates those wealthy sons of bitches*
> *I feel so grand when I tap a wealthy scum*
> *I am Avreyml I am a classy bum*
>
> *(LITTLE BRYNA puts together bra.)*

BIG BRYNA: *Down and out there were times so many*
Begged for bread only poor folks gave a penny
But those fat cats with wallets thick and high
They'd curse at me chase me through the night
He'll be a thief they'd say and they were right
I am a thief but I'm a real great guy

BOTH: *Ich hays Avreyml der faygster marvikher*
A groyse kintsler kharbet laykht und zikher
Just a kid when I landed in a cell
Came out with honors I did very well, Oy Oy
I don't hang out with those other crooks and snitches
I steal from cheapskates those wealthy sons of bitches
I like a gentleman who looks me in the eye
I am Avremyl I am a real great guy.

LITTLE
BRYNA: Oh my God, they're waking up? No…

(Back to the 1970's.)

BRYNA: No… No it looks good. Come on let's try it with a sweater then you'll see. How about these Angora ones? There's only two left. Where's the lady? All right Tybele I want you to take this sweater and go hide it in sporting goods… Go! Twenty-nine dollars are they crazy? Tse lavookhes. All right…

(Tearing a button off the sweater.)

Hello Missus? Yes. You know my daughter she'd like this sweater but uh…unfortunately there's something wrong with it look. One of the nice buttons is missing. Yah. So… No, no it's the last one I looked. So I was thinking maybe you could give us something epes a little off the top? 50% would be good.

(Back to the 1930's.)

LITTLE
BRYNA: Good, Now put it on. Tie it around the back.

BIG BRYNA: Does it fit?

LITTLE
BRYNA: Yes. Let's see.

                (Jumping up and down.)

BIG BRYNA: Ah I don't shake anymore!

LITTLE
BRYNA: Good, now let's make one for me.

BIG BRYNA: As if you need?

                (BIG BRYNA leaves.)

Scene 6—The Campfire

> *(1930's, LITTLE BRYNA settles by the fire under-*
> *scoring into the song "Oy hert zikh ayn".)*

LITTLE
BRYNA: *Oh herts zikh ayn mayne libe mentchn*
              Oh listen carefully to words in my sad riddle
              Fin vanent nemt zikh
              Zukt mir a za groyse vaytig
              And how does so much sorrow
              Fit in one small fiddle

> *(BIG BRYNA enters with army coats, knapsack,*
> *etc. and climbs into LITTLE BRYNA's hovel.)*

BIG BRYNA: Get me some water... *(Cleaning herself.)* Oh no, I
              need moss again...

> *(LITTLE BRYNA pours water into BIG BRYNA's*
> *hands.)*

              You are so lucky you don't need moss yet. You
              know what? I'm starting to get rewards for my
              trouble, ha ha. You want to see what I got?

LITTLE
BRYNA: I'm tired. I want to go to sleep.

BIG BRYNA: Chocolate. Have one. Hey come on, what's the
              matter with you? Look what else I stole after they
              went to sleep. Men they always go to sleep after.

> *(Putting a beret on LITTLE BRYNA.)*

              Look at you, you little partisan fighter. No, no, no
              it's true.

> *(Pulls sheepskin vest out of knapsack.)*

Come try it on. Come on. You look just like Molly Picon. Don't you like that?

Yidl mitn fidl… Arye mitn bas.

LITTLE
BRYNA: *Dos lebn is a lidl…*

BIG BRYNA: Git.

LITTLE
BRYNA: *Ikh vel aykh zugn mayne libe mentchn*
I'll tell you everything
You ever need to hear now
The fiddle cries because
It learns from its musician
About his heartbreaks
His loves and his prayers

BIG BRYNA: Today is not a day to be sad Bryna. Your prayers have been answered.

LITTLE
BRYNA: You don't know what I pray for.

BIG BRYNA: No? But I can teach you a new song.

(*Pulls gun out of knapsack.*)

LITTLE
BRYNA: Where did you get that?

(*Sung as a brokha [prayer].*)

BIG BRYNA: Oh god get me a gun so I can kill the Polish men who torture me.

LITTLE
BRYNA: I don't pray for that…never.

BIG BRYNA: And you tell me why not?

LITTLE
BRYNA: I pray that my mother is still alive…and that the soldiers…that Januk will be good to me.

BIG BRYNA: Oh Bryna, he won't. Bryna he never could be.

LITTLE
BRYNA: He already is. He doesn't beat me anymore. He has a gun and he takes care of me.

BIG BRYNA: And if the Nazis came he would turn you in to save his own soul.

LITTLE
BRYNA: He loves me! He tries to...leave me alone.

BIG BRYNA: Bryna have you lost your mind? Wake up. A Polish Jew-hater lover. Have you told him what your Torah says about that? Listen to me Bryna. There's no reason for us to stay with them any longer. We can take care of ourselves now.

LITTLE
BRYNA: No, we can't. What are you talking about?

BIG BRYNA: We have our own gun, we can leave here tonight.

LITTLE
BRYNA: And go where?

BIG BRYNA: Into the woods further. My father he always talked about Yiddish partisans in the forest, so we'll find them...and you're going to come with me, I won't leave you here alone.

(*Starts to leave through hatch, dragging LITTLE BRYNA. LITTLE BRYNA makes her stop.*)

LITTLE
BRYNA: I can't. I can't. Can't you see Bryna. You're strong but I can't go into the forest without a soldier to take care of me.

BIG BRYNA: Sh sh sh...

(*The song "Still the Night" begins.*)

Still now the night is full of starlight
See how even the frost it burns the land

Do you remember what I already taught you
To hold a revolver in your hand

LITTLE
BRYNA: *I remember what you already taught me*
                to hold a revolver in my hand

BIG BRYNA: *A girl in a sheepskin and a beret*
                A gun clinched tightly in her hand
                A girl with cheeks as smooth as velvet
                Spies on a Nazi caravan

BOTH: *A girl with cheeks as smooth as velvet*
                Spies on a nazi caravan

BIG BRYNA: *She aims, pulls the trigger, hits the target*
                Her pistol, toy-like, small had reached its mark
                A truck full of deadly ammunition
                One shot stopped it in the dark

BOTH: *A truck full of deadly ammunition*
                One shot stopped it in the dark

BIG BRYNA: Here put these on.

LITTLE
BRYNA: You stole their pants? You left them without any
                pants?

BIG BRYNA: Put them on. If the men don't think you're a girl
                then maybe they'll leave you alone. How do I look?

                (Both girls climb out of the hovel and start climbing
                the ladder.)

BOTH: *As dawn breaks she crawls out of the forest*
                Snow white garlands in her hair
                Alive now she glows with this small victory
                With hope for a future free and fair
                Alive now she glows with this small victory
                With hope for a future free and fair

(End of ACT ONE.)

A truck full of deadly ammunition
One shot stopped it in the dark

ACT TWO

Scene 1—The Forest

(*Lights up on BRYNA in chair looking at photo album. Crossfade to LITTLE BRYNA in forest.*)

(*The music for " I Miss My Home" begins.*)

LITTLE
BRYNA:

When I was young
Life was a song
I felt so blessed back then
I always thought if I forgot
I could return again
And now the time has flown
I'm left here all alone
Remembering childhood schemes
How distant they now seem
How long ago I dreamt those lovely dreams

I long to see my home again
Does everything still look the same
That little yard, the tree that grew
The leaky roof a bit askew
I miss my home
Four walls a table and a chair
Yet there was so much there to share
My secret dreams, my youthful song
The only place where I belong
I miss my home

I hear the song
That gentle breezes sigh
With the warmth of a mother's lullaby

Oh how much longer must I roam
For what was once my mother's home
It could be brick it could be loam
It could be straw or made of stone
I miss my home

Scene 2—Cross Piss Story

(BRYNA in 1970's.)

BRYNA: This was my home, Tybele, for five years. This is
           where I lived. You see, a log was my couch...the
           sky...that was my television, and nice green moss.
           this was my bed...soft...warm. Because where
           there's moss...animals they also sleep...and they
           also leave their mess, so not far away...aha you
           see... They sleep there they pish here and you
           know what's growing? Mushrooms. It's not dis-
           gusting. You peel off the skin. Oy Tybele you see,
           in the daytime, Bryna and I we would hide under
           low lying bushes that were thick with leaves. The
           Nazis could build a fire right beside and never
           know we were underneath. At night? We ran, from
           village to village. We stayed off the roads, they
           were too dangerous. Look down the road. Some-
           thing is coming over that hill. Is that a truck, it
           could be soldiers? How do you know? If you see
           something coming towards you on the road what
           you do is you stop. If it keeps moving then maybe
           it's a cow, something else. But if it stops when you
           do, it could be watching you...that's when you be
           careful...you move, the other way across the road
           and stop again. If it follows you? Then quick, quick
           into the forest. But it was better to stay off the
           roads...in the places where the roads cross. What
           do you call it? Crossroads? Yes... It's a dirty joke.
           You see at the crossroads the Poles they like to put
           up crosses so the Nazis they can hang Jews on it.

(1930's.)

LITTLE
BRYNA: I'm staying on the road Bryna. Who would expect
                    Jewish girls to be so stupid to walk in the middle of
                    the road.

BIG BRYNA: All right, let's just get past the cross.

                    *(Sound of danger. The girls are surprised by SS
                    troops)*

LITTLE
BRYNA: Nazis! Oh no!

BIG BRYNA: Yesteshmee Polki! Nyet Jeduvki! We're Polish
                    girls!

LITTLE
BRYNA: Bryna, what are they doing?

                    (The girls are caught and forced up on to the cross.)

BIG BRYNA: They're going to hang us up.

                    *(Men tie them up, play with their skirts and walk
                    away. BIG BRYNA is tied up on the side that can
                    see over the hill.)*

LITTLE
BRYNA: *(Quietly.)* I didn't see them, I'm sorry Bryna.

                    (Looking over hill.)

BIG BRYNA: There's a truck over the hill. It's waiting for them.

LITTLE
BRYNA: Will they just leave us up here?

BIG BRYNA: I don't think so or they wouldn't be lining up on the
                    road with rifles.

LITTLE
BRYNA: NO! Oh no...

BIG BRYNA: Say goodbye little cousin.

LITTLE
BRYNA: *(Overlapping.)* No Mama... Shma yisrael adonai elohaynu adonai ekhad...

BIG BRYNA: *(Overlapping.)* I'm sorry Tata. I told you I wasn't strong enough...and I wasn't smart enough...I'm sorry...

(BIG BRYNA starts to shake.)

LITTLE
BRYNA: What are you doing?

BIG BRYNA: Nothing

LITTLE
BRYNA: You're shaking... Why are you shaking?

BIG BRYNA: I have to pee!

LITTLE
BRYNA: So pee already.

BIG BRYNA: NO. I won't. Embarrass myself in front of them? Not in front of Nazis.

LITTLE
BRYNA: They're gonna shoot us any minute so just go...but stop shaking!

BIG BRYNA: I need to hold on.

(Percussion cue: gunshots.)

LITTLE
BRYNA: Bryna are you shot?

BIG BRYNA: No...are you?

LITTLE
BRYNA: No...

BIG BRYNA: I think the shots came from over the hill.

(Violin plays "Zog Nit Kein Mol" [Never Say].)

It's Partisans! Yiddishe! Jewish Partisans!

LITTLE
BRYNA: Yidn?

BIG BRYNA: Yes

LITTE
BRYNA: Finally, Oh my dear God... We did it, we made it.
              Barukk ato adonai elohaynu melakh haolam, She
              hekhiyanu, ve ki amanu, ve higiyanu, lazman
              haze. [Blessed art Thou oh Lord our God for bring-
              ing us to this season.]

              (Overlap with Hebrew prayer.)

BIG BRYNA: I told you we'd find them. I told you. Not Polish,
              not Russian, but Jewish Partisans!

LITTLE
BRYNA: I can't see!

BIG BRYNA: They've tied up the Nazis. They're bringing them
              back over the hill.

LITTLE
BRYNA: Yidn! Mir zaynen du. Mir zaynen Yidn!

BIG BRYNA: Up here... We're here... Jewish girls!

              (As they are being taken down from the cross.)

LITTLE
BRYNA: Mir zaynen Yidn. Oh yo! Az got zol zugn sis emes.
              [We are Jewish. Oh yes. As God is my witness it's
              true.]

              (The Partisans ask them where they are from.)

BIG BRYNA: We come from Warsaw. We've been looking for
              you since last summer. We've come to join you.

              (Partisans don't agree.)

BIG BRYNA: They'll take us. We're girls with a gun.
LITTLE BRYNA: And we have bullets.

LITTLE
BRYNA: They're not going take us because we're girls.

BIG BRYNA: They'll take us. We're girls with a gun.

                (Pulls out gun.)

                Wait. Varet.

                (Music stops. The Partisans are impressed.)

LITTLE
BRYNA: And we have bullets.

                (The Partisans agree to take them.)

                Thank you God.

                (Partisan theme resumes as they start to march.)

BIG BRYNA: No wait. Please. Don't take them away. Not yet!

                (Partisan theme stops.)

                Hey you, SS… Nice boots.

                (Squats down over the boots.)

BRYNA: *(From the 1970's remembers.)* The best pee I ever had
                in my life.

                (Partisan theme up and out. Shift to 1990's.)

TYBELE: The two Brynas spent more than a couple of years
                in the woods with the Jewish Partisans. They be-
                came very useful to them. Especially my mother.
                She spoke Polish like a Pole not like a Jew. She was
                sent into town to get information for them, medi-
                cine, food. My mother the spy. That's what my
                friends called her. When my girlfriends and I
                would have sleepovers we'd play Matt Helm,
                Emma Peel, Bryna Chudy. My mother was Ingrid
                Bergman and Scarlett O'Hara wrapped into one. In
                school my best marks for writing were when I
                would tell one of her stories. Names changed to

protect the guilty. I came downstairs one Saturday morning and found three of my friends from school listening to mom's stories. Nobody bothered to come get me. She was charming them with stories that I'd never heard. My stories were always so full of pain.

Scene 3—German Boots

>   *(LITTLE BRYNA enters with men's boots.)*

LITTLE
BRYNA: Come on. Let's go!

BIG BRYNA: What are we doing?

LITTLE
BRYNA: I'll tell you on the way. I'm going!

BIG BRYNA: I'm coming.

>   *(Walking.)*

LITTLE
BRYNA: We have to meet them at the dluga ooleetsa. We
                have to wait by the butcher and we have to deliver
                a note.

>   *(Shows BIG BRYNA the note.)*

BIG BRYNA: To who?

LITTLE
BRYNA: I don't know… They'll be here.

BIG BRYNA: You're sure? All right…

>   *(Sound cue: They see danger.)*

Gestapo.

>   *(The girls try to leave but are stopped.)*

No. Yesteshmee Polki. Polki, Nye Jeduvki…

>   *(LITTLE BRYNA drops the letter.)*

To yest list da Moye Matka! It's a letter for her mother.

(The girls are pushed into the interrogation room.) Boote? Dalinam Boote… We were given the boots from the Germans. What do you think? Koorva. Yes we're Polish whores for German soldiers.

(LITTLE BRYNA throws up.)

Look what she gives you Germans. A baby… No. She's too scared to talk. Because we're whores! How else would we get their boots? NO…

(BIG BRYNA is thrown into the chair.)

BRYNA: That's when they took my hands Tybele and…they did to my nails. Ahhhhhhhhhhhhhh! Yesteshmee Polki! Nye Jeduvki! …I watched them go to the corner where the Commandant was sitting and they spoke together in German. I could understand perfectly what they were saying… Then they came back and repeated the same thing to me in Polish. "We'd almost believe you, the tall one with the big mouth, you look like a whore. But look at the little one's nose…" I spit right back… "Look at your commander. He's got a big nose. Is he Jewish?"

(BIG BRYNA is slapped back down into the chair.)

I lost a tooth…but at least they let us go.

(BRYNA in the 1970's, affected by her own memory.)

Oy. I need something Tybele! Get me a glesselle tai. Get me my tea! Good, good… Now go get us some chocolate… No! No not there. It's in the freezer, on the left behind the liver. And get an ice pack for your hand. It looks swollen… Come sit with me. We'll sip tea and eat chocolate. Do you want to go shopping? The black cape you liked, maybe it's reduced. We could see. Here, take a big piece…

Come on. I'm asking you nicely…. It's not the end
of the world. So you're hurt? You want to know
hurt? With everything I lived through in my life I
learned three things. Not to know from allergies,
never to allow myself the luxury of a nervous
breakdown. And number three, get used to it,
Tybele. There isn't one person in your life you'll
meet who won't hurt you.

(Referring to the TV.)

Never mind. Just get me "epes" something on the
TV. Get me a Lawrence Welk… Ah… The cham-
pagne lady. Yup, and I'm the shit lady. I got to go to
that damn bar mitsvah tomorrow with your dad's
family. And look at these damn nails…they don't
grow. You got some colour something I can hide
these nails? Yes, red.

*(Scene is played from the chair while young
TYBELE is doing her mother's nails.)*

Red red red. My mother had red lips. She was a
beauty, never wore a stitch of makeup. Me, I got
my father's nose…don't laugh, you got it too.

(She gently slaps TYBELE's swollen hand.)

BRYNA: I'm sorry.

YOUNG
TYBELE: It's ok. It's just tender. Can I go back to bed now
ma?

BRYNA: You shouldn't have lied to me. You think your
mother's stupid. I wouldn't find out? No matter
what I am…crazy, the worst monster? I'm the only
mother you got. OK go back to bed but turn the
channel… I can't stand it when he waltzes with
that old witch… No, no, no go back… What was
that? The next channel. Tybele, the black and
white, the documentary. Oy Tybele… How I didn't

end up in that pile? You see that? That's Nazi films. They were proud of what they did. Move move…let me see their faces. Let me see a face. Oy Tybele, that's where I should be.

YOUNG
TYBELE: Mommy, why do you do this to yourself every single night you see a documentary. Let's put on a movie OK? Mama! You're not going to find your parents there. It's forty years later ma. If they were still alive, you would have found out from the agencies.

BRYNA: Get the hell out of my sight! You hear me. Move! Get away from me before I smash your other hand.

Scene 4—Lost Child

> *(Opens with the song "Dos Elnte Kind" [Lost Child].)*
>
> *Es yukt mir ver syukt*
> *Und lost nit zu ru*
> *Oh Mame mayn mamelle*
> *vu bist du vu?*
> *Es Zukht dikh dayne Brynyelle*
> *S'ruft dikh dayn kind*
> *S'yomert und S'voyet in feld um der vint.*
>
> *I'm chased, but by who?*
> *They won't leave me alone*
> *Mame, My mammelle*
> *where have you gone?*
> *It's me Bryna, I'm calling you*
> *Brynyelle your child*
> *I searched every field Mama*
> *Through the dark forests so wild*
>
>> *(BRYNA kneels in front of her chair and starts cleaning the floor.)*
>
> Look Mama. Look at this mess that I'm living in?
>
> *My father is gone who knows where he'd be?*
> *The evil that captured him took him from me*
> *The night was so dark when they stole him away*
> *But it's your face mama I remember I remember*
> *still today*
>
> …I don't want to be like this.

Through this burden of day
Through this wandering night
Restless from lack of sleep
Awake full of fright
Oh child mine do you hear it?
Your father's feet coming near
I'm your Mommy I'll rock you
I'll sing you to sleep

Mama!

(Ovelapping LITTLE BRYNA who is in labour.
Back to 1930's.)

LITTLE
BRYNA: Mama!

BIG BRYNA: No Bryna. Sha Bryna shush sha. The Nazis are
              upstairs...you can't scream...

              (To the Partisan men in hiding with them.)

              I'll keep her quiet, I promise... Please. Please.
              They'll kill us all... *(LITTLE BRYNA's water breaks.)*
              I'll clean it, don't worry. I'll clean it but
              sha...shhh...

              (LITTLE BRYNA pauses in labour.)

              You see. It's not so bad.

              ("Roshinkes Mit Mandlen".)

              Unter yideles vigelle
              shtayt a klor vays tsigelle.

              (Another contraction. To the men:)

              Turn around, don't watch... It won't cry... It
              won't. I know.

              (To LITTLE BRYNA.)

              It can't cry Bryna. It can't.

LITTLE
BRYNA: I know.

              *(LITTLE BRYNA has the last contraction. The
              baby is born into BIG BRYNA's hands. To the sol-
              diers:)*

BIG BRYNA: I'll do it. I'll do it.

              *(She unties her bootlace and strangles the baby.
              Gives the baby to LITTLE BRYNA. Digs a hole in
              the earth. LITTLE BRYNA says the Kaddish.)*

LITTLE
BRYNA: Yisgedal veyisgedash shemai rabo, Bealma divra
              khiruse veyimlakh malkhuse, Be khayekhon
              uvyomekhon, uvekhai dakhol bays Israel ba agalla
              uveezman kareev veimeru amen.

              *(The song "Under Your White Starry Heaven" be-
              gins.)*

BIG BRYNA: *Unter dayne vayse shtern*
              Shtrek zu mir dayn vayse hant
              Mayne verter zenen trern
              Viln ruen in dayn hant
              Ze, es tunklet zeyer finkle
              In mayn kelerdikn blik
              Un ikh hob gor nit kein vinkle
              Ze zu shenken dir tsurik
              Un ikh hob gor nit kein vinkle
              Ze zu shenken dir tsurik

              Under your white starry heaven
              Touch me with your pure white hand
              All my words are flowing teardrops
              Placed to rest within your hand
              See they twinkle very faintly
              From my dismal cellar view
              And I crave a peaceful corner
              To reflect them back to you

(BIG and LITTLE BRYNA together. One in English, one in Yiddish.)

Un Ikh hob gor nit kein vinkle
Ze zu shenken dir tsurik
And I crave a peaceful corner
To reflect them back to you

LITTLE
BRYNA: *My Dear God I'd gladly grant you*
Every single thing I own
There's a fire deep within me
And all around the flames have grown
From the silence of dark corners
Martyred cries come piercing through
So I climb the highest rooftop
And I search the skies for you

(BIG and LITTLE BRYNA together. One in English, one in Yddish.)

Loyf ich hekher lber dekher
Un ikh zukh vu bist du vu
So I climb the highest rooftops
And I search the skies for you

BOTH: *Chased through narrow streets and courtyards*
By a world that's gone insane
I pick up my broken bowstring
Sing to you my song of pain
Under your white starry heaven
Touch me with your pure white hand
All my words are flowing teardrops
Placed to rest within your hand

(BIG and LITTLE BRYNA together. One in English, one in Yddish.)

Mayne verter zaynen trern
Viln ruen in dayn hant.
All my words are flowing dewdrops
Placed to rest within your hand.

I pick up my broken bow string
Sing to you my song of pain

Scene 5—Stopping the Tanks

(TYBELE with girlfriends after school, 1970's.)

YOUNG
TYBELE: Ma...can you come here! I'll ask my mom, she'll
                   know. She speaks seven languages. In the war, she
                   went from Poland to Germany...and had to pre-
                   tended she was German.

BRYNA: What are you telling them? You girls you want a
                   drink. So get... And I never stepped foot in Ger-
                   many. Are you crazy? I did go with my cousin
                   north to Russia but...

YOUNG
TYBELE: Oh you'll love this. My mom was with the Yiddish
                   Partisaners...

BRYNA: Partisans! Please Tybele. And we went north after
                   we left the Yiddish partisans...and what's to love?
                   Going north we ran into Nazis... Bryna and I we
                   ran into the forest quick quick into the...um, the
                   guts...the holes... the what do you call? Foxholes?
                   That's it. Into the foxholes that the soldiers built
                   yes? And we're in there and the Nazi comes run-
                   ning right up to us. But it was dark so he couldn't
                   see if we were really inside. He was right above us,
                   but he was afraid to come in. So what did he do? He
                   took his gun and bapa bapa bapa bapa...up and
                   down. One, two...

                   (Referring to bullet holes in her leg.)

                   My medals. Bryna wasn't so lucky either. She
                   ended up with a gash on her cheek from a bayonet.

                   (1940's.)

LITTLE
BRYNA: Do we even know where this road goes?

BIG BRYNA: Keep walking Bryna! We'll never get there if you
                keep stopping.

                (Checking the stars.)

                As long as we keep going north we'll get there.

LITTLE
BRYNA: Are you sure this is north?

BIG BRYNA: The wind comes from the north, that's north, stop
                complaining. When we get to Moscow you'll see
                we'll find my father, and he'll find your mother.
                You can't sleep now. We sleep when it's light. Do I
                have to carry you? Come on... Ah!

LITTLE
BRYNA: I thought it didn't hurt anymore?

BIG BRYNA: I don't feel my leg at all and then it shoots a sharp
                pain. Are you sleeping again?

LITTLE
BRYNA: No.

BIG BRYNA: Bryna, have you looked at your cheek?

LITTLE
BRYNA: No, I don't have a mirror. OW!

BIG BRYNA: It's turning green.

LITTLE
BRYNA: I know. Don't touch it then.

BIG BRYNA: It stinks.

LITTLE
BRYNA: You don't smell so good yourself.

BIG BRYNA: We have to clean it again.

LITTLE BRYNA:	Don't, don't…just don't.
BIG BRYNA:	Let's go down here. I have to find you some moss.
LITTLE BRYNA:	We did that already. It doesn't help.
BIG BRYNA:	All right, then I have to pee on it.
LITTLE BRYNA:	Oh… I'm going to?…No thank you.
BIG BRYNA:	You want your pretty face to be left with a hole in it? Come on lie down and I'll pee on it.
LITTLE BRYNA:	You want me to pee on your leg?
BIG BRYNA:	I don't have pus running down my leg.
LITTLE BRYNA:	You're always peeing on me. I don't want to be peed on.
BIG BRYNA:	Lie down.
LITTLE BRYNA:	No!
BIG BRYNA:	The sun will be up soon. Lie down so I can disinfect it.
LITTLE BRYNA:	I don't want to.
BIG BRYNA:	Are you gonna lie down and let me help you or not?
LITTLE BRYNA:	All right, I'll lie down.
BIG BRYNA:	And don't go to sleep. I pee on it and then we start walking.

LITTLE
BRYNA: Oh God just watch what your doing... Last time...
                it tastes terrible.

BIG BRYNA: Then keep your mouth shut.

LITTLE
BRYNA: You should talk.

                *(She squats over LITTLE BRYNA and tries to pee
                but nothing happens.)*

BIG BRYNA: I need to drink. We need to find a river.

                (Sound of tanks in distance.)

                What's that? Do you hear something?

LITTLE
BRYNA: What?

                (They hide in the tall grass.)

                Russian soldiers.

BIG BRYNA: I told you we were going north, I told you! Hey
                Ryebyata! Boys! Hey Soldata Ruskya... Boys we
                want to come to your country! Open your blouse!
                Smile to the soldiers.

LITTLE
BRYNA: I know. Hey! Boys!

                (Lifts her skirts and whistles. The tank stops.)

BIG BRYNA: Moscva da, Pejalsta.

                *(BIG BRYNA opens the hatch to the tank as
                LITTLE BRYNA climbs in.)*

                Come Bryna come, up in to the tank...spaseeba.

LITTLE
BRYNA: Thank you.

Scene 6—Moscow

(1990's.)

TYBELE: I love telling the story about my mother going to Moscow. Two girls in the bottom of a cramped tank with six very horny Russian soldiers. And Little Bryna keeps sticking her pussy cheek in to the soldiers faces until they finally leave them alone. It was a long way into Moscow and all the girls talked about was going to the Kremlin. So one of the soldiers took pity on them and escorted them on the subway all the way into the heart of Moscow. To Red Square...right to the front gates of the Kremlin. And he leaves them there with bread and enough money for a subway ticket to get out of Red Square. And what did these two girls do? Their first night in Moscow. They took the only money they had in the whole world and went to see a Cary Grant movie. Days knocking on the doors of the Kremlin and nights spent wandering the streets.

(In a crowded square, 1940's.)

BIG BRYNA: Eez vyeh nyee tye? Excuse me, is this a line for food?... For Lenin?

LITTLE
BRYNA: A line up for Lenin! Isn't he dead?

BIG BRYNA: He died the year I was born. Follow the line.

(As they follow the line into Lenin's tomb:)

LITTLE
BRYNA: Unbelievable. We're not waiting to stare at a dead person, are we? Bryna, it's not proper to look at the dead and at least in the forest we didn't have to wait in line.

BIG BRYNA: Are you coming?

(*The line stops inside.*)

LITTLE
BRYNA: That's Lenin? Why do they keep him like that, under glass? He looks so small.

BIG BRYNA: He was a big thinker.

LITTLE
BRYNA: How do they keep his boots shiny? I wonder if he smells?

BIG BRYNA: He's the father.

LITTLE
BRYNA: The father is dead... Let's go.

(*Both leave the tomb.*)

BIG BRYNA: When we find my father I can tell him I saw Lenin.

LITTLE
BRYNA: What if we don't find him?

BIG BRYNA: Stop it! How can you say that? Don't I go to the Kremlin every day?

LITTLE
BRYNA: And every day they tell you the same thing. Your father is not here. They don't know your father...they don't care about your father.

BIG BRYNA: And everyday I get in a little further—another door, another office, another diplomat.. You'll see. I'll find the right diplomat and...

LITTLE
BRYNA: And then you'll get us both killed...

BIG BRYNA: You have no idea who my father is.

LITTLE
BRYNA: Can we just find a place to sleep tonight?

BIG BRYNA: What, the police station isn't good enough for you?

LITTLE
BRYNA: Everything is upside down with you. We promised
                the police sergeant one night and it's already a
                week. He won't let us in again...

BIG BRYNA: You think he'll get away with that with me? I'm
                Mordche Chudy's daughter. Besides, I think he
                likes you.

LITTLE
BRYNA: I can't anymore Bryna. I just can't. I want to go
                back. I want to go home.

BIG BRYNA: You have no home.

LITTLE
BRYNA: Poland is liberated. We can go back.

BIG BRYNA: I am going to stay here until I find my father. You
                go where you want... This time I won't stop you.

LITTLE
BRYNA: Won't you come with me? ...Bryna?

                *(They move away from each other. Both sing "Vu
                Ahin Zol Ikh Gayn".)*

                Vu ahin zol Ikh gayn
                Ver ken entfern mir?
                Vu ahin zol lkh gayn
                Az farshlosn yeder tir?
                S'is di velt groys genug,
                Nor far mir Is eng un kleyn
                Vu ablik, Kh'muz tsurik
                S'is tseshtert yede brik
                Vu ahin zol Ikh gayn?

                Always hounded and chased
                Uncertain of each day of each place

BIG BRYNA: *Living in the blackest of night*

LITTLE
BRYNA: *Hoping when there's no hope in sight*

BOTH: *Surrounded by only foes not one friend*
              Is there no one on whom I can depend

BIG: *Tell me where should I go*   LITTLE : *Vu ahin zol Ikh gayn*
     Who will answer my plea   *Ver ken entfern mir?*
     Tell me where should I go   *Vu ahin zol Ikh gayn*
     When every door is closed to me   *Az farshlosn yeder tir?*

B&G:*In a world that's so large*   *In a world that's so large*
    Is there no place for me so small   *Is there no place for me*
                                                 so small

B&L:*Every day I'm turned away*
    Is there no place for me to stay

BIG: *Tell me where should I go*   LITTLE: *Vu ahin zol lkh gayn*

B&L:*Vu ablik, Kh'muz tsurik*   *Vu ablik, Kh'muz tsurik*
    S'is tseshtert yede brik   *S'is tseshtert yede brik*
    Tell me where should I go   *Tell me where should I go*

TYBELE: My mother smuggled herself into Paris on the top of
              a train. Little Bryna, she studied in a Polish Univer-
              sity, and eventually moved to Israel. It was years
              before my mother travelled to visit her. On the trip to
              Israel, on the airplane, my mother stole the miniature
              silver cutlery from her dinner tray. But wait, the best
              part is that in the dark during the in-flight movie, this
              "gentleman" that was sitting next to her he forgets
              where he is and starts to...play with himself. I mean
              I would have just died. But not my mother. No, with
              one hand she reaches up and pushes the call
              button...with the other hand she slowly reaches
              down for her purse. She waits until she sees the stew-
              ardess coming down the aisle and then pulls out the
              knife and screams, "You don't put it away mister
              you're gonna lose it." ...I love that story.

              (TYBELE exits.)

Tell me where should I go
Who will answer my plea

Scene 7—Israel Wedding

> *(1970's. An older LITTLE BRYNA enters as mother of the groom.)*

LITTLE
BRYNA: Mazel Tov to you too. Thank you. You should live to enjoy at your son's wedding as well. Oy gotenyu she's here. Nathan come... Oy...

> *(BRYNA enters dressed for the wedding.)*

How beautiful you look Bryna.

BIG BRYNA: Shalom.

LITTLE
BRYNA: Shalom...

BIG BRYNA: It's thirty years Bryna and you didn't get any taller?

LITTLE
BRYNA: And your mouth?

BIG BRYNA: It's not smaller.

> *(They laugh. The bride and groom are hoisted on chairs.)*

LITTLE
BRYNA: Come I want you to meet my son and his bride. Oh, careful up there. Put her down...be careful...

BIG BRYNA: You'll fall!

LITTLE
BRYNA: Aren't they beautiful? Nathan. This is my cousin Bryna all the way from Canada. All right. All right later. Come we'll sit down.

(To the children.)

LITTLE
BRYNA: Ikh hob dir a zoy lib. I love you very much. And
              you Rochele, you too. I love you, I love you. Aren't
              they a beautiful couple?

BIG BRYNA: You still make me sick with your lovey dovey.

LITTLE
BRYNA: What's the matter you don't feel good? You need a
              drink?

BIG BRYNA: Nothing's changed huh? Love, love, love, no mat-
              ter what with you, everything is always love?

LITTLE
BRYNA: It's a wedding.

BIG BRYNA: Love is for other people, not for me.

LITTLE
BRYNA: What about your Frenchman? You have love?

BIG BRYNA: I have nothing is what I have. Oy Bryna when I met
              him with his seven brothers and sisters. Can you
              believe it? Seven of them they all got through the
              war not a scratch. Like idiots they just walked
              through the war.

LITTLE
BRYNA: Smart idiots.

BIG BRYNA: Peasants, that's what they are! My Tata had more
              culture in his little finger. He'd be so ashamed. I'm
              glad he's not alive to see.

LITTLE
BRYNA: You know? When did you find out?

BIG BRYNA: Yesterday I went to Yad Vashem. They found a
              foreman who used to work for my father.

LITTLE
BRYNA: In his factory?

BIG BRYNA: Yes. He told me what happened when they went back.

LITTLE
BRYNA: Back?

BIG BRYNA: To Warsaw. My Tata, my father he made boots for the Nazis. And he was alive Bryna right until the end... They came...they opened up the floorboards, took the women to the trains. They told the men to stay. But my father, he went running after the train. My mother, her head half out the window waved him back...! Go back! Go back Mordche. Stay! Save yourself. But no! Wasn't I alive? Couldn't he have stayed for me?

LITTLE
BRYNA: He didn't know.

BIG BRYNA: He chose to go with her?

LITTLE
BRYNA: At those times you do things...you don't think. It was just in his heart.

BIG BRYNA: Bryna, he went to the ovens. He didn't have to.

LITTLE
BRYNA: No one should have had to... We did things all the time...we didn't think...

BIG BRYNA: He didn't think about me. Why didn't he think about me?

LITTLE
BRYNA: You don't know what he was thinking.

BIG BRYNA: The truth is nobody ever thinks of me. Even you, you never really cared for me.

LITTLE
BRYNA: What are you talking about? Bryna, it's a wedding. I'm sorry it's so hard for you.

LITTLE BRYNA: We did things all the time...we didn't think...

BIG BRYNA: You're sorry? I'm glad you're sorry. But where
                were you when I needed you to be sorry, huh?
                When I needed you to help me to get out of my hell.

LITTLE
BRYNA: What are you talking about, not the reparations?

BIG BRYNA: Yes the goddamn reparations.

LITTLE
BRYNA: You wanted me to lie and say that you were in
                Dachau and not the woods?

BIG BRYNA: Yes, goddamn you, yes. All you had to do was to
                write a simple letter . Tell them what I told you so I
                could get more money.

LITTLE
BRYNA: But I had already told them already the truth.

BIG BRYNA: And God forbid Miss Goody-Two-Shoes you
                should lie to the Nazis!

LITTLE
BRYNA: Why do you need to exchange one hell for another?
                It isn't enough?

BIG BRYNA: And who's measuring you? You tell me when did
                my life become enough?

LITTLE
BRYNA: Bryna don't. The first time we see each other in
                how long and is this what you want to say to me?
                You have love…you have a family, a daughter…

BIG BRYNA: You can take your goddamn love and you can keep
                it.

LITTLE
BRYNA: I can.

BIG BRYNA: Yes. The one thing I needed you to do for me. What
                I did for you? Was that enough?

LITTLE
BRYNA: Yes I know. You did for me.

BIG BRYNA: Everything I did for you. You wouldn't have made
                it except for me.

LITTLE
BRYNA: I know...I know.

BIG BRYNA: And so now it's enough. You don't need me and I
                don't need you. It's finished. It's a wonderful life
                and to hell with you!...

Scene 8—The Grocery Store

> *(1990's.)*

TYBELE: After mom came home from Israel she was always angry. Even in the store back in Calgary, the grocery store. She'd get so mad at the little kids just coming in to buy penny candy.

> *(1970's.)*

BRYNA: How much money you have? Come on open up. Show me the hands. Five cents? What the hell are you doing making all my candy dirty?...This is all you can take. A couple of green spearmint leaves and a black nigger baby... Now go.

YOUNG
TYBELE: Mommy, they're not nigger babies, they're called black beauties.

BIG BRYNA: All right. *(To the child.)* Go get out of here! Shoo!

> *(Welcoming a lady customer.)*

Bonjour Madame. Comment ça va? Ah oui? ha aha. C'est vrais...il fait très beau. Yes I love the chinooks. Remember the Stampede the year it snowed on the morning of the parade and remember the shnook, it came right in... *(A customer enters.)* Oh hello. Just a minute mister... Oui Madame, le lait c'est au dessus dans la frigidaire. Oui? ...ce's ça... All right. What, you want the bread? Dat's sixty-nine cents. Dat's enough. Hmm? A bag? You know what? The bags cost me two cents. The bread's already in a bag. You're gonna walk home just like that. Tybele, go get me a tit from the

back, a #7, a #9, a couple of tits. Yes? Tit... It's a bag,
What do you think?... What language? What language do you think?

("Bryna's Song" begins.)

My friend you ask where I come from
Is my accent so hard to place?
Come on, guess me
Figure me out now
I beg you
And I'll try not to laugh in your face.

You don't know what I am
And I like it that way
Madame est-çe que tu es Française?
Oui, je suis French I could say
Or maybe a little bit Polish
Da, proshe, Jinque-ee, a Polski too

In dreyed
Oy Oy I'm not a Jew
No sir not for you
You don't like my accent
Not good enough for you
My friend to hell with you.

What do you think that I am?
No, I'm not from Iran
Russian? Could be
German? That's me!
A question comes to my mind
What are you deaf dumb and blind?
Hindu? Zulu? Shihtsu? Yoo Hoo!

In dreyed
Oy Oy I'm not a Jew
No sir not for you
So you think I'm a Heinz 57?
My friend to hell with you.

You don't tell them anything. It's better that way

They find a way to hurt you with things that they say
The ones who say they're friends, how they love to betray
Smile their gentile smiles pretending everything's OK
But watch out for their blaming lies come Xmas day
With Jew this and Jew that it's a constant replay
Of a nightmare I've already lived ten times today
And I'm tired of all you bastards, so please go away
Tybele, you don't trust nobody

In dreyed
Oy oy I'm not a Jew
No sir not for you
You think that I speak with an accent?
It's you that listens with an accent
My friend to hell with you too!

You want a bag with that? ...Merry Krats mikh.

(Scratches her arm.)

Am I right?

Scene 9—Israel

(1990's into 1970's.)

TYBELE: If my mother was right then the only place I'd ever feel safe as a Jew would be Israel. Hell, I can feel safe in Calgary. But you know I loved going to Israel. When you get off the plane in Israel there's like a sea of short green men in army uniform with big hands... Hey hey hey...Bli adayim... the first thing I learned...without hands. Please talk to me without hands. They loved this ass. I was once offered two chickens and a donkey for this thing. The second thing I learned was, EFO autobus? Well I had the address of Little Bryna and I wanted to go see her. I got on a bus and took a three-and-a-half hour trip out of Tel Aviv into the desert. We got to this desolate place. Nothing but tall apartment buildings sprung out of nowhere. And I get off in the parking lot like she told me and there she is... God, Mom was right. She is short.

            (LITTLE BRYNA enters carrying a bag of groceries, puts them down, 1970's.)

LITTLE
BRYNA: Bryna?

TYBELE: Tybele.

LITTLE
BRYNA: Oh of course... Oy, look at you. Just like your mother, oh my. It's so good to see you, you made it here all right?

TYBELE: Yes.

LITTLE
BRYNA: You must be hungry. Why don't you come
                home?... Oy look at you.

TYBELE: Oh no, here. I'll take it.

LITTLE
BRYNA: Thank you...come on. So, the flight it was long?

TYBELE: Oh Bryna, it was amazing. I've never been on an El
                Al flight before. No elevator.

LITTLE
BRYNA: You get used to it.

TYBELE: You sleep all night, but then in the morning they
                open up the blinds and this hot Mediterranean sun
                comes streaming in and you see jet fighters flying
                in on both sides. A Rabbi stood up and started
                davenen and everyone started applauding and
                singing. I'd never seen anything like it before in my
                life.

LITTLE
BRYNA: Good, you want something to drink? Excuse me.
                Oh...

                (LITTLE BRYNA takes off her shoes.)

TYBELE: What's wrong with your feet?

LITTLE
BRYNA: Nothing, I just have very close veins.

TYBELE: If you have varicose veins then why do you wear
                high heels ?

LITTLE
BRYNA: Oh, my Willie. He likes them. I like them too. So tell
                me Bryna. Oh no. I'm sorry. I can't help it, her nose,
                her mouth.

TYBELE: I have my mother's face.

LITTLE
BRYNA: It's a handsome face. So tell me Bryna. I'm sorry.

TYBELE: It's OK. You can call me Bryna if you want.

LITTLE
BRYNA: How is your mother? Is she happy?

TYBELE: Oh... She's like she always is.

LITTLE
BRYNA: And...uh Grisha? Things are better between them
              yes?

TYBELE: She sleeps on the couch.

LITTLE
BRYNA: Oy.

TYBELE: She has for a long time.

LITTLE
BRYNA: Your mother you know, she was always angry,
              always hard. Funny sometimes, but always hard...
              You want some mandel broit? I made it.

TYBELE: I'd love some.

              (LITTLE BRYNA exits to the kitchen.)

              You know my mother told me a lot of stories about
              you and her and about the time you spent together.
              But there's some things that I don't know. Bryna,
              remember that time when you were both hiding in
              a basement of a farm house in with the partisans,
              and the Nazis were upstairs and one of you went
              into labour...

              (LITTLE BRYNA enters.)

LITTLE
BRYNA: You know about that? How do you know about
              that? Your mother she told you about that?

TYBELE: You know what she didn't tell me Bryna? Whose baby was it? Was it your baby or was it my mothers?

LITTLE
BRYNA: What difference does it make? So you have children, a boy?

TYBELE: I have two, a boy and a girl.

LITTLE
BRYNA: You see how the world gives back... You have a husband?

TYBELE: Ma says no khupee, no shtupee.

LITTLE
BRYNA: So he's Jewish?

TYBELE: Oh boy... My first boyfriend was German and my second was Lebanese.

LITTLE
BRYNA: Ya?

TYBELE: Mom didn't talk to me then for six months.

LITTLE
BRYNA: Oh? No!. You know my Nathan when he got married, he married Rochelle a beautiful Jewish girl. But you know, I would have loved her just as much if she was an Arabishe, a Shvartse. Epes... OK, maybe not a German, but Egyptian?

TYBELE: How can you even say that... How?

LITTLE
BRYNA: How? Tybele...how can I not learn from what Hitler did to me. Hatred is a horrible thing. You love, that's...

TYBELE: That's enough.

LITTLE BRYNA: Hello! Down in front!

LITTLE
BRYNA: Always. Listen you want to go to a movie?

                    (The song "New York, New York" starts playing.)

                    My favourite movie is playing.

TYBELE: An Israeli movie?

LITTLE
BRYNA: Oh no, NO, NO, *New York, New York* with Liza
                    Minelli! Come on. And afterwards I'll show you
                    around.

                    (They walk out on the street.)

                    Stay close. Your mother used to drag me around by
                    the nose, now I'll drag you. Come on. Oh it's so
                    crowded already. Excuse me.

                    (They settle at the theatre.)

TYBELE: Oh my God. Why's everybody screaming?

LITTLE
BRYNA: What screaming!

                    (Screaming across the theatre.)

                    All the way from Canada she's coming!

TYBELE: Bryna, why are there three rows of subtitles?

LITTLE
BRYNA: Ya, ya... There's Yiddish, Hebrew...then some-
                    thing Arabic.

TYBELE: Arabic? How do you know what's going on?

LITTLE
BRYNA: It's in English?

TYBELE: But I can't see it and I can't hear!

LITTLE BRYNA:	Hello! Down in front!
TYBELE:	Bryna! There's a man sitting next to me with a rifle.
LITTLE BRYNA:	It's a guard. Don't worry. He's a Sabra. Forget it! *(To the guard.)* She's new here.
TYBELE:	Ahhhhh! There's a chicken in the theatre!
	(The song "For All We Know" begins.)
LITTLE BRYNA:	My cousin's daughter from Canada. She's beautiful... Oy, here it comes. I love this song.
TYBELE:	Are they always quiet for songs?
LITTLE BRYNA:	This one anyway.

> *For all we know*
> *It may only be a dream*
> *We come and go*
> *Like a ripple on a stream*
> *So love me tonight*
> *Tomorrow was made for some*
> *Tomorrow may never come*
> *For all we know*

BOTH:

> *For all we know we may never meet again*
> *Before I go make this moment sweet again*
> *We won't say goodnight until the last minute*

LITTLE BRYNA:

> *I'll hold out my hand*

TYBELE:

> *And my heart will be in it*
> *For all we know it may only be a dream*
> *We come and go and go*
> *Like a ripple on a stream*
> *So love me tonight*
> *Tomorrow was made for some*

(TYBELE steps on to chair platform to become:)

BRYNA: *Tomorrow may never come*
For all we know

(Song "Telling Stories". TYBELE sings to chair.)

TYBELE: *You've told me your stories for so many years*
And still the telling has only begun
These stories half hidden in memory and shame
They've fought to survive and they've won
You've told me your stories in clear black and white
But I know there's more, more than one way to see
There are shades of bright colours in shadow and light
There's a rainbow inside of me
Mama I'll tell the stories
Mama I'll hold my head high
Make you the heroine you always should have been
Mama I'll show the world why
You've told me your stories, I'll never let go
Though fragments keep drifting and fading somehow
I know what I see every night in my dreams
It's my turn to tell the stories now

(TYBELE sits in her mother's chair.

The End.)

Song List

Act One

Telling Stories (Dertsaylen Mayses)
Lyrics by Theresa Tova and John Alcorn
Music by John Alcorn
© 1997

Mayn Shtetele (My Little Town Belz)
Lyrics by Jacob Jacobs (1892–1972)
Music by Alexander Olshanetsky (1892–1946)
English translation by Hindy Nosek-Abelson and Theresa Tova
© Ethnic Music Publishing Co. (New York)

Oy Mame Bin Ikh Farlibt (Oh Mama Am I in Love)
Lyrics and Music by Abraham Ellstein (1907–1963)
© 1941 Ethnic Music Publishing Co. (New York)

Yidl Mitn Fidl (Yidl with His Fiddle)
Lyrics by Itsik Manger (1901–1969)
Music by Abraham Ellstein
From the Molly Picon film *Yidl Mitn Fidl*
© Ethnic Music Publishing Co. (New York)

Puttin On the Ritz
by Irving Berlin
© 1928, 1929 by Irving Berlin
Copyright Renewed. Int'l Copyright Secured.
Reprinted by permission. All rights reserved.

Vi Shlekht Und Vi Biter (How Hard and How Bitter)
Collected from Sara Rosenfeld of Montreal who heard it in the
Yiddish Theatre in Warsaw before World War II. First published in
1959.
English translation by Theresa Tova

Geshem Nign (Autumn Prayer)
A Hebrew prayer that laments be ill-prepared for winter.

In Krayuvke (In a Hideout)
Originally by Hench Kon (1898–1972)
Adapted by Partisans from the songs *Shpil Zhe Mir a Lidele* in Yiddish
or *Yiddish Tango.*
English translation by Theresa Tova and Hindy Nosek-Abelson

Avreyml Der Marvikher (Avreyml the Pickpocket)
Lyrics and Music by Mordechai Gebertig (1877–1942)
One of the last Yiddish Folk Poets. Among the most popular in Eastern
Europe and throughout the Yiddish world.
English translation by Hindy Nosek-Abelson and Theresa Tova

Oy Hert Zikn Ayn (Oh Listen Carefully)
Lyrics by Itsik Manger (1901–1969)
Music by Abraham Ellstein
From the Molly Picon film *Yidl Mitn Fidl*
English translation by Hindy Nosek-Abelson
© Ethnic Music Publishing Co. (New York)

Shtil Di Nakht (Still the Night)
Writen by Hirsh Glik (1922–1942) after Partisans blew up a German
convoy. Glik was imprisoned in a concentration camp and killed by
the Germans.
English translation by Theresa Tova
© Congress for Yiddish Culture Inc. (New York)

Act Two

Ikh Benk Aheym (I Miss My Home)
Created in the Vilno Ghetto
Lyrics by Lyb Rosenthal (1916–1945) who wrote for the revue theatres.
Drowned by the Nazis in the Baltic Sea near Konigsburg.
English translation by Theresa Tova
© Congress for Yiddish Culture Inc. (New York)

Dos Elnte Kind (The LOnely Child)
Lyrics by Shmerle Kaczerginski (1908–1954) who, after the liquidation
of the Vilno Ghetto, became a Partisan fighter.
Music by Yankl Krimski
English translation by Theresa Tova
© Congress for Yiddish Culture Inc. (New York)

Unter Dayne Vayse Shtern (Under Your White Starry Heaven)
Music by Abraham Brudno who was deported to a concentration
camp where he died in 1943.
Lyrics by Abraham Sutskever (1913–), a well-known Yiddish poet
and writer before World War II. It was first presented in a play in the
Vilno Ghetto theatre. After the destruction of the ghetto, Sutskever
joined the Partisan forces. He lives in Israel.
© AKUM Publishing (Israel)

Vu Ahin Zol Ikh Gayn (Tell Me Where I Should Go)
Lyrics by S. Korntayer, a Yiddish actor, who died in the Warsaw
Ghetto in 1942. Written before the war, it became popular in displaced
persons camps and in the ghettos.
Music by Oscar Strock or Zigmund Berland
Paris © 1949 Feldman Ltd. (London)
English translation by Hindy Nosek-Abelson and Theresa Tova

Bryna's Song
Lyrics and Music by Theresa Tova and John Alcorn
The translation for "In Dreyed" is "Go to Hell".

For All We Know
Lyrics by Sam M. Lewis
Music by J. Fred Coots
© 1934, Cromwell Music Inc. (New York)

Telling Stories (Dertsaylen Mayses)
Lyrics by Theresa Tova and John Alcorn
Music by John Alcorn
© 1997

Acknowledgements

I do not intend *Still the Night* to be a factual account even though it is full of many truths. Against the onslaught of nay sayers and revisionists, it is vitally important for the next generation to find its own truth. This play is inspired by my memories, my dreams, my nightmares. These are my truths and no one else's.

I would like to thank the family of people who supported the development of *Still the Night*. To Anne Anglin for her unwavering faith, Liza Balkan for her breath of life, Mary Kerr for her genius, John Alcorn for his impeccable musical taste, Tom Diamond for just being the best, Claire Hopkinson for her calm wisdom, Wayne Strongman for his diligent care, Hindy Nosek-Abelson for her friendship, and Melanie Joseph for being my teacher. From the incredible *Still the Night* fundraising committee, to the granting bodies and theatre who leapt on board, my leap of faith has been supported by so many.

Special thanks to Adam Austin, Pnina Zilberman, Arron Fainer, Helen Zukerman, Paul Falzone, Chana and Joseph Mlotek, Bret Werb, Adrienne Cooper, David Duclos of the Theatre Centre, Claire and Wayne of Tapestry Music Theatre, Susan Serran of Theatre Passe Muraille, Michael Dobbin of Alberta Theatre Projects, Paul Thompson, Joan and Ray Bird, Svetlana Zylin, Bill Humenick, Hannah Havlicek-Martinek, Barry Lipson, Rick Feldman, Barbra Linds, Michelle Landsberg, Maurice Paperny, the Willie and Lea Kohn family, the Ontario Arts Council, du Maurier Arts, The Canada Council for the Arts, the Laidlaw Foundation, the Zuckerman Foundation and all my supporters and friends.